Farewell

Clay

Dove

poems by

Sophia Falco

UnCollected Press

Contents

I. Levitate

II. Higher

III. Suspend

IV. Revive

For those traversing through darkness, may the light be
strengthened from within.

I. Levitate

Hourglass

The sand in the hourglass is missing
though the glass is not shattered.

I discover the tan grains scattered
in my green porcelain bathtub.

I decide to let the water flow from
the silver faucet, and the sand swirls.

The crystal-clear water is too
transparent so I add blue dye.

I create an ocean, and when I shut
the faucet off, time sinks back to the bottom.

Crimson Dove

The eyes of a crimson dove quiver,
the sun washes out the color
of its feathers from crimson to pink
like the melting pink ice cream
with clear sprinkles it is eating
on the burning black pavement.

(Sugar crystals sparkle.)

I witness the pink dove
levitate and float
upwards like
a pink balloon
into the blue sky.

"POP!"

The man shot it.

Golden Rays

The man on the moon shoots
the sun, some golden rays
fizzle out.

The darkening sky
does not deter me from
walking my tiger in circles
on the cracked wooden floor
in my yellow bricked
apartment.

(Red leash bedazzled with rhinestones.)

I sigh creating a void,
orange and black stripes
disappear—
remaining rhinestones.

I pick up each sparkling
jewel and arrange
them in a star.

Drifting

This stunning crimson feather
       drifts effortlessly
in the hot summer sky,

          and defies gravity
     with each passing
       minute.

I pluck this treasure midflight
     with my thumb
and index finger.

         I long to display this beauty
    in a little plastic box
      to add to my collection,

but instead, like a lone
    escaped flame,
it burns me.

Marble

I hold a green and blue
swirled marble in
the palm of my hand.

This fragile sphere
is a miniature
earth—I am larger
than life.

Infinitesimal Stars

I shrink stars small enough
to fit in my faded brown
treasure chest in my closet.

Equipped with my butterfly
net I capture them as they fall
from the heavens.

I quickly lock them up,
and they jounce against
the wooden walls.

The frame becomes illuminated,
and as I rejoice,
I lose the key.

Snowflakes

I wish for my thoughts
to be as wonderful
as snowflakes.

I hope to witness them
from behind the window
freefalling towards the ground
in the crisp breeze.

I long to catch one
on my fingertip.

Besides, Raging Tiger, You Can't Just Go Asking For Mercy
*after Kaveh Akbar

Besides, raging tiger, you can't just go asking for mercy.
With claws like that, it's easy to grasp

onto prey—but even with dewclaws
you cannot write words. It's as if you illegibly scribble

with red ink in the snow. I do not touch red pens
because they are cursed. New problem:

perhaps you are blessed and provoking violence is just in
your nature. Or, you are cursed whereas

I am not violent, but once I succeeded at hurting myself.
Do you feel pain when burrs get in your paws? The tiniest

injury could lead to something monumental. Tiger, tiger
please do not burn bright. Know who you are, you're not

a star, instead follow their light from the heavens.

Time

The invisible inner workings
of my mind are like many
clocks moving backwards
as darkness approaches
the hands quickly fade away—
time is nothing but a memory.

Imagining 42 Tiny Scuba Divers

Bubble rings like misplaced
angel halos arise within
my teardrop from tiny
scuba divers the size
of pinpricks swimming
about aimlessly with salt
coating their masks,
and high on painkillers.

II. Higher

The Battle Within

My words are shooting stars
with no filter flying rapidly
like demons in the sky,
the ego soars drenched with sorrow.
The air is funny today.

> Molecules bouncing around
> so rapidly, so many multiplying!
> I can see them.
> The wind pushes me, and I fall
> some more even though I'm lying

on the red brick patio
under the hot sun
while my thoughts are running
towards yesterday,
and sprinting towards the future.
My mind is wandering like a

> lost soul.

Crowded:
seconds
minutes
hours.

> A cover song about love is on repeat.
> Hours pass and my shirt
> is soaked with sweat
> mixed with hot tears.
> I know I am as good as God,

13

Picasso is in my back pocket
no one knows who lives behind
these curtains,
not even I,
how hard I try,
I don't want to be forgotten.

Pollen

The pollen coats
my fingertip
like gold,
but with a
single
blow
this
vanishes.

Yellow Blinds Me Into Oblivion

The sunflower stands like a skyscraper
roots like a spiderweb on steroids
its seeds the size of pinpricks
yellow blinds me into oblivion.

Roots like a spiderweb on steroids
my feet get tangled in the silky strands
yellow blinds me into oblivion
I pass out.

My feet get tangled in the silky strands
I witness the grandiosity of nature
I pass out
nature wins like it should.

I witness the grandiosity of nature
its seeds the size of pinpricks
I pass out
the sunflower stands like a skyscraper.

Lead Mare

A herd of black horses
disperse in every direction,
and gallop at the speed
of light in my continuous
nightmare permeating darkness.

This darkness travels
throughout my entire being.

This darkness eclipses
my soul.

This darkness unjustly taints
my mind.

Whereas I long for my mind
to be as pure as a field of
purple wildflowers
where my thoughts are free
to roam like joyous
golden horses,
but you set the flowers
on fire and shot
the lead mare
in her heart.

Longing To Time Travel

I wish I could
hopscotch across
the upcoming months
without stepping on the white lines, but
I wouldn't prevail
with each jump my tears would
blur up
the chalk.

Dusk

At dusk the demons
consume the hues
of pink, orange, and red
that streak the
horizon like messy
paintbrush strokes,
but what remains on the
corner of their mouths
is the color red
like lipstick
or blood.

Don't Whisper

27 emotions are written
on these blank cards, but
no kings, no queens, and no jokers.

I construct a house, but even
a whisper of truth
will collapse these walls.

Stigma And The Spaceship

Society is sun-tanning its stigmas.

Twisted with ignorance
the man on the dusty street
shouts:
"YOU ARE BIPOLAR!"

I desperately desire to respond,
but now my tongue
is coated with despair,
and I'm unable to speak.

It was as if I ate *sour patch kids*
that were drowned in hate,
and I am dying to spit
this taste out on him.

My soul shrinks and is scorched
by his weapon of choice
his shout:
"YOU ARE BIPOLAR!"

His words ring in my mind
as if a metal gong was hit
42 times with the force so strong
that it shattered this goldness.

Bipolar disorder does not define
me, and that is why I am defiant
to those three words as if they
are in fact larger than the moon.

I wish I am on a spaceship to escape
that very twisted attitude, and watch
over earth the way a monk watches
over dew drops on a green piece of grass.

Blades Of Grass

A magnificent hummingbird crashes
in a lonely meadow
where sharp blades
of grass are tinged
with her blood—
sorrow is too heavy
for the tiny winged bird
to carry on her back.

Pinwheels

Purple clouds spin like pinwheels
I shoot my crimson arrow
droplets burst my soul falls with them
still my ego is drenched with sorrow.

I shoot my crimson arrow
I am high as that child's kite
still my ego is drenched with sorrow
my sigh of relief with every beat, my heart.

I am high as that child's kite
my reflection is muddled in that puddle
my sigh of relief with every beat, my heart
a tiger butterfly cries.

My reflection is muddled in that puddle
droplets burst my soul falls with them
a tiger butterfly cries
purple clouds spin like pinwheels.

Sandcastle

It is the size of a penny
this miniature sandcastle.

I kick it, and send particles
upwards in the troposphere.

They do not travel far.

III. Suspend

My Therapist Pleaded Me To Imagine A Placid Lake

"Imagine a placid lake"
my therapist pleaded me,
she needed me to calm
down because mania
had taken over my mind.

I just could not
failure—
the ideology behind it
felt incomprehensible as fish
spewing fire.

Terrified,
I saw a
raging
and
threatening
waterfall
that burst
with
psychedelic colors
and radioactive
waste killing
all living
organisms
in the plunge
pool.

The man from the dusty street,
he continued to shout:
"YOU ARE BIPOLAR!"
all while I was sitting
on her purple couch.

Hopes Of Freedoming From A Psychiatric Hospital

For fourteen traumatic days
"pulse check"
I know we've only lived
together for a short amount of time
bipolar disorder
I've seen you in the movies
Silver Linings Playbook
bunch of Hollywood propaganda
pushing agendas to romanticize you
not everyone gets restraining orders
"pulse check"
I remember the ambulance ride
told the driver to turn up the music
"pulse check"
mania, you brought me
up up up
"pulse check"
countless medication to
try and bring me
down down down
"pulse check"
an injection too
"pulse check"
hopes of freedoming
and to touch the blue sky
because it felt like rainbows
were catching on fire.

Rocket Ship

I condensed the power of the ocean
into one single droplet of water,
it was my hot tear that warped time
during my fourteen day stay
in the psychiatric hospital,
my body no longer
felt like mine—
oh mania.

My nurse told me to paint every day,
art therapy she said,
but I could only paint
countless red rocket ships
that I longed to escape
on to connect my body
to my mind
that was somewhere
lost in space
and threatened
by a black hole.

(I could feel she was disappointed in me.)

I taped up each identical
painting
to my wall
just to realize
that part of me
was still on earth.

Spaces

There is a space
between
the two words
"outer space"
therefore
the space
between
outer space
does exist,
and so there
is free white
space while
white is
the color
of the
sun.

Flashlight

I condensed the power of the sun
into one single beam of light,
I kept my flashlight hidden
under my bed in the psychiatric
hospital during my fourteen day stay,
it set aflame the ending
to my fairytale—
oh mania.

My nurse told me to read
picture books every day,
and she even took my flashlight away,
but I could only witness
the sun rise
and the sun set
from my little window.

(I could feel she was disappointed in me.)

Instead I cut out
all the pictures
of the suns
in the stories
and made a collage
of one giant sun,
and realized
that part of my soul
was still shining.

Mania Strikes Noon

You'd visit me when mania strikes noon
stuck in a tiny hospital room.

The world was mine,
but I didn't make it in time.

Seconds
minutes
hours
collapsed
on my head
so I hid
under
the white sheets
on my bed.

a prison
      a prison
            a prison

Depression talks back, don't you know?

Whereas reality crumbled at my fingertips
like
a stale sugar cookie Depression

      talks back to me, don't you know?

And you
you love
me always—
just the same.

A Letter From My Dear Friend

*I know mania strikes noon, I can't stop worrying about you.
You, stuck in a tiny hospital room. This does not say
anything about who you are as an individual because
ever since the day I met you, you are you. Not a stale sugar
cookie disintegrating by madness. Please, I'll talk back to
Depression for you—I truly don't care for it, Depression!
In fourteen days then you will be granted free. Don't you
understand? I love you. Bipolar disorder does not define
you, and I love you. Definitions and diseases don't please
me. I know you two lived together for a short amount of
time, but the intensity built and built like my ever
increasing love for you. You are you.*

IV. Revive

The Realm Of Blue

I find little credence among
my defeatist thoughts,
and they are now fleeting
like the salt being lifted off
the ocean in the crisp breeze
lost in the realm
of blue
sky.

Letting Go

I throw all my rocket ship
paintings into the cool water.

I witness the tide snatch
them up, and carry them
off into the vast blue ocean.

Revival

That golden horse leaves
a trail of light in the field
of invincible purple
wildflowers,
and she gallops faster
and faster illuminating
the way to freedom.

Caught In A Spider Web

A leaf dangles upside down
like a trapeze artist
floating to and fro.

A leaf spins
quickly and tightly
like a ballerina.

A leaf twirls
like an umbrella
whose top is inside out.

Around The World

I dribble my prized possession
on the cracked blacktop
surrounded by redwoods
to the beat of a lyricless song.

My basketball is faded orange,
a setting sun.

I play *Around the World*
and I make every shot.

Replay.

Imagining 200 Tiny Astronauts

I imagine a dried dandelion
flower as the new frontier.

The core is a miniature
space station,
and each seed
is a lovely astronaut
where the white fluff
are their space suits.

(They are tethered down.)

Whereas the wind
comes as a divine
intervention.

These tiny astronauts
disperse in every direction.

They have arrived
at their destination.

This destination
is the freedom
to soar
in this present
moment.

Yellow Leads Me To Enlightenment

I traverse through serenity
countless bright petals mimic the stars
this field of sunflowers brings joy
yellow leads me to enlightenment.

Countless bright petals mimic the stars
my body is relieved from sorrow
yellow leads me to enlightenment
my mind experiences freedom.

My body is relieved from sorrow
my spirit soars like the blue jays
my mind experiences freedom
I witness the wisdom of nature.

My spirit soars like the blue jays
this field of sunflowers brings joy
I witness the wisdom of nature
I traverse through serenity.

Envisioning A Clay Dove That Takes Flight

I was given a miniature clay dove
to be my guardian the day
living with bipolar disorder
became my reality.

I placed her on my bedroom windowsill
as a reminder that there can still be peace
despite my struggles that ebbed and flowed
like waves crashing on a shoreline.

She rested in the same spot for a decade
though every morning I'd check on her
since I longed for her to take flight.

(I would dust her off with a tiny scrap
of a green dish towel.)

She became more than my guardian,
in fact, she manifested my hopes and dreams—
I too wanted to soar.

Her motionless presence filled up
my bedroom though this fine morning
she was no longer there.

It was as if she came to life,
and snuck out my cracked window
without a sound during
that hot summer evening,
and took flight under the bright stars.

At first I was heartbroken at this loss
yet I became conscious of my inner strength,
and that what is constant is change.

Ode To A Sunflower

In outer space a strong
sunflower floats in orbit,
and a lovely astronaut
sprinkles joy
on this sunflower.

The sunflower's seeds light up
in a yellow spiral,
one by one,
rapidly!

Beams of light
radiate out from each seed,
and the petals pulsate
with power.

(Flashes of gold in the
realm of dark matter.)

These beams of light
reach the earth
coated in a blanket of black,
cutting through the darkness;
zigzagging like lightning.

Oh, how the sunflower shakes its head
like a lion shakes his mane and showers
            yellow pollen
that floats, drifts, and coats
the darkness ever so
gracefully with gold ,
like a rain
that reaches earth.

A sunflower bringing
joy into this dark world!

Farewell

When we parted, all the water
evaporated from the earth's ocean
so only endless mountains of salt
remained as heavy as the moon,
as heavy as my heart.

On a pilgrimage in your honor
to discover the tallest mountain
I traversed through treacherous terrain
while the sheer sun against the white
hurt my eyes, and with every heavy footstep
my black boots crunched the salt
where this sound ricocheted
from mountain top to mountain top.

I prevailed by reaching the sparkling summit
then laid flat on my back, and made an angel
sensing her spirit rising
while witnessing the pinnacle of the sunset
its pink rays like roses without thorns—oh how
I wish I could have bottled up that for you.

For the sake of freedom, I shouted:
"LET IT RAIN!" well equipped with
my lifeboat made out of driftwood.

The rain did come dissolving the mountains,
and I saw your reflection in a singular drop.

With gratitude for those who have stood by my side with unwavering support during this sometimes challenging yet beautiful journey of mine called life.

Acknowledgments

Thanks to the editors of the following publications where these poems first appeared:

"Farewell", Winner of Mirabai Prize for Poetry: *The Raw Art Review* & nominated for a Pushcart Prize
"Imagining 200 Tiny Astronauts" in Top 10 Finalists for WD Nature Contest: *Wingless Dreamer*
"Besides, Raging Tiger, You Can't Just Go Asking For Mercy" after Kaveh Akbar anthologized in *Nasty Women: In Celebration of International Women's Day* by *Moonstone Arts Center*
The Raw Art Review:-"Flashlight" (forthcoming)
The Raw Art Review:-"Infinitesimal Stars" (forthcoming)
Indolent Books: "Hourglass"
Indolent Books: "Longing to Time Travel"
The Closed Eye Open: "Marble"
The Closed Eye Open: "Don't Whisper"
The Write Launch "Imagining 42 Tiny Scuba Divers"
The Write Launch "Drifting"
The Write Launch "Sandcastle"
Tiny Seed Literary Journal: "Envisioning A Clay Dove That Takes Flight"
Tiny Seed Literary Journal: "Snowflakes"
Tiny Seed Literary Journal "Yellow Leads Me to Enlightenment"
The Silent World In Her Vase "Letting Go"
Poets Choice "The Realm of Blue"
Poets Choice "Time"
Creative Release Magazine: Foothill College: "Lifeline" now titled "Around the World
The Beautiful Space: "Pinwheels"
The Beautiful Space: "Dusk"
The Beautiful Space: "Pollen"

The Immortal Sunflower, a short chapbook containing some of these poems was published by UnCollected Press in December 2019 as a winner of *The Raw Art Review* Poetry Chapbook Contest. Within this chapbook all poems were published prior:

"Red Dove" a runner-up for the William Wantling Prize: *The Raw Art Review*

"Rocket Ship" 3rd place in *Poetry Matters Project* Literary Prize 2019 (college category) & published in *The Esthetic Apostle*

The Beautiful Space: "Hopes of Freedoming from a Psychiatric Hospital"

The Beautiful Space: "My Therapist Pleads Me to Imagine a Placid Lake"

The Beautiful Space: "A Letter from My Dear Friend"

The Festival Review: "Mania Strikes Noon"

Stigma Fighters: "The Battle Within"

Tiny Seed Literary Journal: "Caught in a Spider Web"

The Raw Art Review: "Yellow Blinds Me into Oblivion"

The Raw Art Review: "Stigma and the Spaceship"

The Esthetic Apostle: "Golden Rays"

The Esthetic Apostle: "Ode to a Sunflower"

Praise for the Poetry of Sophia Falco...

"Sophia Falco is a talented, imaginative, driven, raw, crafty,and original poet whose writings overcome and transfigurethe stigma and challenges of bipolar disorder in well- crafted poetic forms that communicate and manage the heights and depths of her being-in-the-world. *Farewell Clay Dove* tracks the levitations and journeys, the loneliness, terrors, illness, as well as the poetic wonder of her journey to health, autonomy, and bliss in imagery of, crimson doves, golden hours of sunset, shrinking stars, hospitals, rocket ships, radiant horses, sheer mania at noon. It is a work of wholeness, honesty, psychic quest, and probing intelligence."
>   —Rob Sean Wilson, University of
>   California at Santa Cruz

"At its finest, poetry contains multitudes, an infinite depth within a few short lines. The poems contained in *Farewell Clay Dove* have an intriguing simplicity that harmonizes with their richness. These poems show remarkable insight into the Falco's subjective world."
>   —Maya Highland, editor of *The Closed Eye Open*

"Farewell Clay Dove candidly accounts the pain, perseverance, and strength that encompasses the bipolar experience."
>   —*International Bipolar Foundation*

"Sophia Falco's world is a dreamy land of swirling colors - until it is upended. *Farewell Clay Dove* is a meditation on mania, when every levitation brings an inevitable fall. The contrast between idyllic nature scenes and harsh reality propels the book forward on a wave of bright color and intense perception. Dandelions become astronauts and skyscrapers grow roots, as the speaker moves in and out of

50

reality, and eventually into the psych ward, where they must confront the workings of their own mind. *Farewell Clay Dove* is a heartfelt and surreal portrayal of what it means to be bipolar."

—Syd Shaw, *Tiny Seed Literary Journal*

"Sophia Falco's new book is wonderful! In reading you will see her progressing toward a powerful revelation. Each section can stand alone, but have more power because of her progression into awareness. My favorite section is "Suspend". The poems here are highly visual. Sophia Falco is very brave."

—Lucinda Clark, founder of *Poetry Matters Project*

Bio:

 Sophia Falco is a faithful poet since she finds poetry essential to her understanding of the universe. Her poems appear in *The Raw Art Review*, *The Poetry Matters Project*, *Wingless Dreamer, Tiny SeedLiterary Journal*, *Indolent Books*, *The Beautiful Space* among other journals. She is the author ofher award-winning chapbook *The Immortal Sunflower* (UnCollected Press, 2019), the winner of the Mirabai Prize for Poetry, and was nominated for a PushcartPrize. Furthermore, Falco graduated magna cum laude along with the highest honors in the Literature Department at the University of California, Santa Cruz. Her Bachelor ofArts degree is in intensive literature with a creative writing concentration in poetry. She loves to take long walks on thebeach to be in the presence of the water, and to witness the ocean's vastness, blueness, and beauty.

Made in the USA
Middletown, DE
18 October 2021

50571158R00035